STARTLING

'Linda France's *Startling* manages to be both expansive and precise, braiding intimate observation with dazzling scope. The collection is hopeful and yet full of the terror of climate collapse, time-travelling and yet absolutely of, and speaking to, the present moment. This is a poet "refusing to collude / in the lie / of simplicity": ecological in her thinking, and rooting her vision into the vast web of connections and complexities behind our trembling, fragile world.' SEÁN HEWITT

'*Startling* is a search for awareness and conviction, a response to alarm, and a determination to understand what alarm means. This remarkable book of poems is both an immersion in the consequences of societal insensitivity to environment, and also in the splendours of existence. There is a vegetal sensuousness and entwined awareness of mutability, vulnerability and persistence that grows into a statement of resistance and hope. Further loss need not happen, and this work – one of technical gusto and virtuosity – is part of that conversation and action.' JOHN KINSELLA

'*Startling* is a radiant vision into the mysteries of deep time and the dizzying minutiae of the present moment. Simultaneously grave and yet full of redemptive beauty, it is both elegy and urgent awakening, shot through with the poet's "lucid hope" for the future.' NANCY CAMPBELL

'Like the poet Bashō, France's poems are alive to the immensity of the moment, subtle to the pressures and urgencies of a greatly disturbed world. The result is an inversion of the elegiac – engaging a deep attention towards hope for a future. These poems feel urgent, essential, and will ask their readers to return to them.' SEAN BORODALE

STARTLING
Linda France

**NEW WRITING
NORTH**

First published in 2022
by New Writing North
3 Ellison Terrace
Ellison Place
Newcastle upon Tyne NE1 8ST

with the assistance of
Faber and Faber
Bloomsbury House
74-77 Great Russell Street
London WC1B 3DA

Typeset by Hamish Ironside
Printed and bound by CPI Group (UK) Ltd, Croydon CR0 4YY

A CIP record for this book is available from the British Library

ISBN 978-0-571-37902-6

10 9 8 7 6 5 4 3 2 1

For Una, Freya, Gwen
and those who come after

CONTENTS

IT'S TIME, HE SAID, TO BURY
OUR DEAD HORSES

For who will we be without being with you
For the distance between our skins splits open
For time has quickened and hearts have slowed
For the world has widened, borders closed
For knowing your flanks in the pitch of night
For remembering you and our wild galloping
For no one speaks of going forward or back
For we count our love in coiling breaths

For horses, horses will inherit the earth
For we sing to you grazing your field of stars
For you were born of the nature to be dust
For a hundred hooves are storm and thunder
For our dream breaks, breaks cantering home
Here on your charnel ground we'll sow a meadow

LE TEMPS

I

It is only in ashes
that a story endures
only the extinguished persists

> I begin the day
> over and over again

ice by the gate
you slide and fall
in slow motion

> puffs of steam
> wet logs on the hearth

watching a poet
walk on TV
curiously soothing

> a week's worth of post
> on the doorstep

windblown snow
lifted like sand
lands like feathers

> the lapwings are back
> that remembered longing

at half past eight
his body is burnt
I light a candle

       we are those men
       on *Terror*, on *Erebus*

each fleeting twinge
attributed
to yesterday's jab

       yes, says Siri, *that's right,*
       everything's fine

O

refusing to collude
in the lie
of simplicity

       a beginning that hasn't
       even begun to begin

when all the clocks stop
she sends me a globe
with a second hand

       one minute sun
       one minute hail

twenty-nine years
in the same house
a long root

    at the dawn of a new world
    we make hands out of clay

doing the crossword
in the middle of the night
Petrol in France (7)

    an hour on the step
    talking about nothing

the places I deceive
myself exposed –
a crack of light

    under the church tower we remember
    what it is to be together

making the impossible possible
the possible easy
and the easy elegant

    behind the poem's lines
    the lungs of the wind

O

red moon
over Massachusetts
awake all night

  IPCC Synthesis Report
  subheading: *Deep Uncertainty*

what stays
are sensations
not sentences

  a single email
  and the whole day is lost

abrupt downpour
so strident
I can't hear the car radio

  walking over the bridge
  between then and next

all that you touch you change
all that you change changes you
the only lasting truth is change

  storm picking up
  over Jam Tree Gully

slowly
the two of us
make haste

in Pakistan, smog
a fifth season

when he dies
he wants his body
to be eaten by bears

new growth on the hawthorn
mizzle falling upwards

O

Gwen carries her own placard
I don't want to live
on a spaceship

what you give the forest
the forest gives you back

I plant eight buddleias
hoping for a summer
astonished by butterflies

defrosting the freezer
is today's weather

all the little suns
on my glasses
raindrops

> more a question
> of when than if

our culture
written in snow
and the planet's on fire

> everything racing
> Wile E. Coyote legs

seven days
without power
a raw stillness

> on the short day's back
> the long night

trailerload of logs –
alder, Matt says,
burns hot

> this will end
> this will carry on

IMMEASURABLE

I

For the duration of this poem, imagine
behind your belly button, coiled, retractable,
you carry a tape measure, passed down from your mother.
Inside its ergonomic case
(a little snail shell world), the tape lies sleeping.
If you tug its silver horn to draw it out,
you'll see the laddered markings of inches inching
and fractions fractioning along a quivering
length, metric and imperial. For the duration
of this poem, all mass, all amplitude, let's
call them years or months, days, or those ever-shrinking
minutes you spool out recklessly, as if your tape
(like nothing else on earth) had no end to its tail.
On the contrary, one day the mechanism
will fail, give up, its measuring contract over.
And, snapped back, that's the full extent of your imagining.

In a world of second chances, what if
those dark spaces behind your navel, in your gut,
were your brain's hollows, the only centre
you knew (and the whole ravelled tangle of you)
so, with your mother's milk, you learned it held
the whole world too? Wouldn't you sense more
deeply the beat of time? Beneath your skin,
within your breath? Might you measure it better –
all the time and all the world that was given
you, trusting that it's all connected – a set
of, let's call them, interlocking boxes
for keeping things, and giving them away?
What if, in this world of second chances
(which is, let's be honest, our last
chance) you chose to act as if it were true?
(Which it might be.) Imagine, what then?

MOORING

Because there's nothing else
   to be done, I step outside
      breathe into the horizon.

Because today there's so little
   to hold onto, I count
      the pylons crossing my eyeline

trace the wires between them
   patchworked fields and trees
      white windmills on the farthest rise.

Because after all I'm here
   I breathe in the wide expanse
      feel my body realign

tissue and bone, all the precious
   nothing, everything I can set my heart
      on, the back and forth of air

a rope braided between being.

TREEINCARNATION

What if you came back as a sycamore –
    aerodynamic on the runway
        of earth and air. Touchdown
for the buzzard, laser-eyed, angelic,
    on your highest branch. Starlings' beaks
        silhouetted in your leafless arms.
Dressed in green, splashing shade for heat-numbed sheep.
    Watch nothing happen but birds, creatures,
        weather. Everything you are not, couldn't
exist without. Rising like a thought
    in the mind of a field that'll take
        lifetimes to reach its conclusion.

    Winged seeds carried home by the wind.

CONKER

From this more-than-half-dark, I don't know
what's on the outside (*random spikes,*

russet brown, three sets of slack lips –
a tree urchin, unstrung, beached).

Whatever gossips there may be
stay silent while I'm here inside

rattling softly like a child
testing the world before springing

into it. I smell of Bulgaria, earth
and honey mixed. My first home

is womb or saddle, ferrying me across
to wherever's next. I suppose

our bones are the same colour – coffee,
yogurt – my shell and me.

It's fed me belonging, freedom,
trust – horse lore I'll bring into the world,

unshod, unbridled, inborn treeness.

SPANISH CHESTNUT

Like the tree it fell from, the fruit
contains multitudes. Soft as a nest,
sweet as a warm glass bauble,
it'll prick your fingers with a thousand needles.

Bring it indoors and inspect
its well-defended carapace,
learn its wintry rhythm, how everything
has a seed and a fruit, like this, in one shell.

The tree's a wild squat creature,
all folds and openings. It wears
its five hundred years like grizzled pelt,
waterfall of wood – impossible to trace

where one thing begins and another
ends: knotted branches, ruffled bark,
lichen, moss and fern, dimples, burrs,
the fresh cut ends' raw concentric circles.

The trunk, which is many trunks, rises
from a rusty ring of rotting chestnuts
striking back into the earth – a clock
of its own making. It'll take more years

than this tree's seen to shed all the grief
you carry in your bones. Peel open
the spiky case to find two sweet nuts
squirrelled together in the plush-lined core.

Like the heart's chambers, they spiral
between life and that dark you can't see
beyond, the endless stretch of time you must pass
on to the future for her safe-keeping.

THE HOUR OF THE ROWAN

A drowned watch loses eighty-six thousand seconds
every day but the time of berry and fishbone green
has an unlocked door for a heart. The tree keeps
taking her jumper off and putting it back on,
a flushed gif. Days cluster and ripen on the end
of thin stalks – their fierce gloss, tight with juice, scratches
your throat. A robin ticks in her branches, grizzled
lichen furring her bones. No word for *end*.

This rowan knows nothing but radiance – her whole
task simply being rowan. She doesn't waste her
mornings scrabbling for words, labouring to calm
her red fury. Nothing left to lose, you climb inside her
and sky is ocean, earth eaten by fire.

Being rowan is brazen, quickbeam, fruiting,
shedding, bird's nest and washing line. Seconds become
minutes become hours, months, years – the memory
of mountains inside her, ash and eagle feather –
safe against calamity, lightning bolts.

LIGHTNING STONE

Origin unknown

You bring me yesterday in a stone
fifty million years old. Formed
from the outside in, fossilised
mud bubbles fused, calcite, aragonite,

coated in limestone, with ruched pouches
and soft folds, it could be a pillow,
your tender turtle shell, carrying
the planet on its back. Or the lost tooth

of a dinosaur I could lay next to
my weary head and dream of – what?
Fire and ice, dragon's eggs, a world
turned upside down while I sleep.

No one knows its exact source –
desiccation, expansion, earthquake,
fracture. The cool surface, fine
as sandpaper, might be this earth

seen from a long way off – fields, rivers
and roads cut through soil, clay, rare
and precious minerals, sister stones
that have seen all weathers. It's too big

to hold in one hand; too heavy and deep
its story of time – the weight of change,
this long waiting, slow patience you brought
me yesterday millions of years ago.

STONE CURLEW

I watch the way you want to reach the end
before you've begun. Here there is only this

egg and our sitting in shifts to keep it warm,
at the mercy of weather, another bird's hunger.

Trust me, you must go to unknown places
and stay inside your body while you try. Look at me

being bird. Why is being human so hard?
I see you – fragile, fierce. What if every single day

was your only chance of incubating what wants
to be born and that was all you had to do – *be there* –

what you were made for, enough to make a stone sing?

THE CUCKOO AND THE EGG

Inside the cuckoo's call, the ear of spring.
Inside the ear of spring, the swaying reeds.
Inside the swaying reeds, the warbler's nest.
Inside the warbler's nest, the cuckoo's egg.
Inside the cuckoo's egg, the eye of gold.
Inside the eye of gold, the tug of the sun.
Inside the tug of the sun, the bird's wings.

Inside the bird's wings, five thousand miles.
Inside five thousand miles, a vast Sahara.
Inside the vast Sahara, the overwintering.
Inside the overwintering, the hunger for young.
Inside the hunger for young, the earth greening.
Inside the earth greening, the heart's sap.
Inside the heart's sap, the cuckoo calling.

ECHOLALIA

Is the bat   night

or is it

       weather

I listen

         to the sounds

it's echolocating

      I can't hear

for a signal

         flicker

of air   and   skin

    of wing

flinch   when it dips

      not in fear

but because I love it

            (her or him

won't cover it)

less than a handful

       of fur   bone

       myth

all   my   human

       atoms   attune

to   our ears

antennae   whirr

       click

in the dusk   you

       articulate

cut   with your

       little knives

silhouettes

yes   billets-doux

WOODLAND MANAGEMENT

Someone's woven a doll-sized hammock among
       the branches by the side of the path, woollen
           strands so unexpected and neat I almost
       weep. A mending, a stitching together
of the Sitka spruce and the humans who planted
       them so near the long straight road where cars pass
           too fast. Further down there's a shrine – faded silk
       flowers and a plaster Madonna where
someone died. I swallow the aftertaste
       of exhaust, mixed with the musk of deer
           who take shelter in this hilltop coppice.
       Conifers can outgrow the men who plant them,
bark a map of forgiveness, universe
       of resin and roadlessness, roots reaching
           out to wrap themselves round their neighbours.
Another time I find a love note tucked between
       the scales of a trunk, blue biro kisses
           kindled into origami, wildfire.

HEARTH

Because she knows my affinity with bone, land's lost and found,
when she lit upon it, dew still cooling its grooves, she brought it
home for me across the border.

She brought it like bounty – a huntress who's never lifted a bow –
and now it lives on my mantelpiece, a candelabra
of calcium, chiaroscuro, as long as my arm,

furrowed crown, five years old. Four arcing tines – another snapped
off, volcanic, cratered – point toward their crepuscular twins
trapped in the antique mirror.

The peaty bark of its underside has stayed unscoured by winds,
arctic storms. A flower blooms where it fell from the stag's brow,
one fat bone eye ringed with toothy petals.

When she brought me his antler, she also brought the deer,
his red pelt and heathersweet hooves, his lost velvet,
haunches' heft, the air of the glens

in his nostrils, still twitching, and the heart's roar from far
far away chambered inside a tufted chest – and see, there
she brought me the whole world.

THE BURNING HOUSE

When a single recurring thought caught
like paper under magnified sunlight,

flames licked their lips and devoured
windowsill, knick-knacks, curtains, chair;

the whole room blackening into one
enormous grate. The towers of books tinder,

tumbling into clips from the end of the world;
all words incinerated till nothing

of Babel was left but grey flakes
of lost imaginings. The stairs turned

into orange scales, flanks of a dragon,
and the chimney roared. Last to go was the bed,

belovèd refuge. In the end, even it was powerless.
By morning all that remained were shadows,

coils of wire. This is what we came home to;
for the first time felt air open through us, pure

as the water that couldn't put the fire out,
strong as the earth deep in our bones.

Heartbeat by heartbeat, life began,
shimmering at the oasis of its conflagration.

TEN TRUTHS

1.

Every day begins with a rise
that's really a spin, a turning.

2.

On 19th July 2021, the Met Office
put out their first Amber Extreme Heat Warning.

We misconstrue what amber means.

3.

We are children of the sun.
Because it came into being,
we came into being,
born from rock and water.

4.

No one speaks the language
of the sun. Egyptian, Aztec

or Anthropocene,
needled with sweat,

we worship or tremble
ninety-two million miles apart.

5.

Such carcinomas
are almost never
a danger to life.

6.

A goddess became the sun,
her grandson the emperor
and he framed her on his flag.

Heart of the solar system,
all the other planets, asteroids,
comets revolving around her.

7.

A sun's day is twenty-five times
longer than ours. Enormous.
Unconquerable. History told us
it made us in its own image.

8.

The summer of 1976
was a blaze of hosepipe bans,
A-level results and packed beaches.

You weren't in your body at the time
so it was a surprise when your skin
turned red and bubbled with blisters.

9.

Once you flew east
and caught up with a second dawn.
The day began all over again,
everyone watching a different film –
            Chocolat, Mission Impossible,
            O Brother, Where Art Thou?

10.

The truth is the best treatment.
The scalpel and nothing but the scalpel.

You are scarred.
You are scared.

How much you love the earth
and the day's eye, the year's.

How close it feels.

GIANT SEQUOIA

Natural History Museum
(Acquired 1893)

Here, at the top of the stairs, we're very small
and very new beneath you, heads tipped back
to read your origins – numbers on a station clock –
analogue seedling in 557, Common Era.

If you were a cake, there'd be twelve pieces,
one for every month sliced through the seasons
your sequoianess saw in her one thousand
three hundred and thirty-five evergreen years.

They called you the Mark Twain tree but rumours
of your death are not greatly exaggerated.
A timeline tells us halfway through your life
Buddhist monk and mathematician Yi Xing

made the first clepsydra, a water-stealing clock,
when just 200 million humans lived in your shadow.
Two deep hollows at opposite poles float like islands
on a map or glaciers melting in a vast ocean.

Variously, you are the colour of tar, coffee beans,
good garden soil and, where the light catches, my father's eyes.
Your bark's ridged like railway sleepers on train tracks
across America where everything's on the move now

and it's hard to know how much space we can occupy
when the earth no longer has room for a gentle giant,
mandala of wood, atlas of the imperilled world,
shield against the weather: *le temps* – the word

used for time too in many languages other than
this one, a wafer on my tongue, dissolving.
I swear I can smell the forest where you were felled –
ancient and piney, earth's incense rising.

DEAD MEN'S FINGERS

After the funeral, I lie down
among the long purples; lower myself in
as if into water and green rises around
me, raindrop and cuckoospit laced between

stalk and seed hoard. Ants and small insects crawl over
me – a felled trunk. This is the nearest
I've been to myself all year. Level with
my eyes a spiral of chimney sweep moths graze on

sprays of pignut. Yellow vetchling tendrils through
bedstraw and speedwell. Further off
shy tufts of cottongrass puff across
a stretch of birches. Even when the sky mottles above

us, I want to stay, becoming, like the orchids, more inside,
animate, haired and stippled, roaring beyond
the line that keeps us separate towards
the tangled loops solstice opens beneath

us, this feral cat's cradle. Flies, zigzagging down,
articulate moist air, these brief lives we're held within,
as I breathe the spicy smell of death and wet sex among
all the gorgeous everything that comes up from under.

INCUNABULA

There are words and then the end of words.
Food no longer taken, nil by mouth.

           She is making something new on a bed of ash.
                A negotiation of wet and dry.

Form and hollow.

           She needs to be low,
               under,
               down,

where the sounds are smaller and can crawl into her ears.

She will forget her own name.
Like a gourd.
Like an embryo, the red tent of the womb.
Like a babe in a cot.
Like a woman in labour.
Like a crone on her death bed.

                        In her coffin,
                          on a pyre,
                          in the oven,
                        under earth,
                        on the water,
                   back to her mother.

Her grave goods are beautiful scars;

her body, a hollowed-out canoe, a shawabti;
her vulva, a fish.

Her amphibian nature.

Water dragon,
bird woman,
urn woman,
cave woman,
avatar,
warrior,
wrapped in leaves for a shroud.

Nothing is an accident.
Everything is an accident.
She will die between everything and nothing,
where she lived all along.

She will be fired into clay,
become her own final creation.
She is going home to the unsaid.
Her thumbprint, dust in the clay.

LE TEMPS

II

You give me a word for this
shimmering, the heart's weather

driving into Newcastle
as if we were travelling
to Samarkand

how to feel sad
without being sad

spiked with caffeine
overnight snow
dreaming yourself into existence

bars of rain
on the sitting room window

one more winter
the same larches
an untranslatable decade

the flowers don't know
it's November

out at sea
all night long
a blue moon

nothing blowing
against nothing

every year
her body
remembers his birthday

two hours lost
in charcoal, pencil, ink

our first visit back
to the cinema
1968, Chicago

O

light the fire
burn the day away

another Monday
uncertain
how to begin

sunlight you want
to call miraculous

filling the day from end
to end so there's no room
for nothing

who of us
is ever ready?

slow Sunday afternoon
watching *Casablanca*
you sob on the sofa

2.30 p.m. around the brazier
autumn equinox

a moment knows
something's almost over
but not what it is

pale lines of rain
against the ploughed field

I paint the stone rise
in the kitchen
a shade called Thunder

listening to Meredith Monk's *Book of Days*
time stops

stay with the ragged joy
of ordinary living
and dying

O

       the day you were born: balancing
       pebbles on a burnt tree

rain non-stop
the garden jumps up
to catch it

       the longest day
       stripped back to nothing

the only yellow flower
on the gorse bush
a yellowhammer

       the here and now
       and the mental there and elsewhere

the yard white
a sudden shower
of sky stones

       on top of the Iron Age fort
       we see beyond ourselves

without water in the taps
your mind full of nothing
but water

distilling time impossible
I try anyway

other names: Hattie's pincushion
masterwort – *Astrantia*
our morning star

you die
you are still here

a few seconds lag
between our chat
connects || separates

O

don't blame the swallows
for your tears

storm moon and hailstones
I warm myself
at her fire

your prayer flags unfurl
windhorses galloping

punctuated equilibrium
how earth evolves
in sudden ruptures

every day the same
every day different

my driver knows
hardly any English but says
we need more water

in ceremonial kimonos
they look back from the future

do not stand
in a place of danger
trusting in miracles

our molehills
are mountains

weather forecast:
new* things*
under* the* sun*

a dead man's tattoos –
fail we may, sail we must

on the windowsill
a bowl
of borrowed time

. . . our perfunctory observations on what kind of day it is, are perhaps not idle. Perhaps we have a deep and legitimate need to know in our entire being what the day is like, to see it and feel it, to know how the sky is grey, paler in the south, with patches of blue in the southwest, with snow on the ground, and the thermometer at 18 [°F], and cold wind making your ears ache. I have a real need to know these things because I myself am part of the weather and part of the climate and part of the place, and a day in which I have not shared truly in all this is no day at all.   THOMAS MERTON

STONE MEADOW ORBITAL

The Weather Clock

Sometimes we know something is wrong but can't tell what it is. Sometimes we know exactly. The year started with a flooded kitchen, a broken boiler, and enough snow to block the road in both directions. The atmosphere in the house was freezing. It smelled of decay; my whole body braced against it.

I was trying to think about the future, but the present demanded my entire attention. I remembered someone saying winter is by far the oldest of seasons; it tenders age upon our memories, taking us back to a remote past. I wanted to bring more of myself into the real, so whenever I could I went outside to look at the snow. The landscape transformed, I was living in a medieval book of hours. I was pressed between the pages of history.

When all our ways of knowing warmth disappear, what do we become? Who?

I wrote in the snow with a stick to make time visible. The surface was icy, hard to penetrate. I had to write in capital letters, which were impossible to think in. The curves were difficult, just as imagining the future is difficult. S O S. Although it looked like one, the snow wasn't a blank page.

Everything felt broken. More men than I'd seen in months came in ones and twos. They said the drain could be unblocked, the pilot light reignited; there would be warmth again.

The past and the present became the future. And it was simpler than I thought: more real, more possible. This is not about me. It's all about me.

We live inside the weather, and it is a clock we carry inside us.

for the first time
the meteor visible
in meteorology

Hope is the Thing with Petals

You're not sure when it started – a habit that grew into a need: hanging a blanket at your window to stop the morning light waking you too early. As if the day didn't belong to you, or you to it. Would you rather sleep than live?

When you were young, puppyish, impulsive, you were better at beginnings than endings. The mechanism inside your body has recalibrated with age. Under cover of darkness, the psyche prepares itself for death. Although you've looked into the eclipse of large finales, as with the blanket you hang up at your window, light has a knack of spilling round the edges. For every ending there's a beginning.

'Endling' is the word used to denote the last surviving creature of a particular species. When they die, that species becomes extinct. Unable to save them, and blind to the irony, we have given our endlings human names as we count them out of the ark: Martha, Benjamin, Celia, George – passenger pigeon, Tasmanian tiger, Pyrenean ibex, Pinto Island tortoise.

I have taken to counting what I want to call 'Startlings'. They are creatures who, sensing their species is facing extinction, feel the cell-tingling impulse to evolve and ensure their survival. Within their tissue and bones, hearts and minds, they enact the necessary transformation. For every Endling there is a Startling.

They are springing up everywhere, like snowdrops, first flowers of the year. How often do you see a single snowdrop? Don't they grow in drifts, in flocks, and spread across great stretches of land, despite extreme weather and human interference?

After a month of snow and frost, snowdrops are pushing through the cold soil, the flowers starting to open. The light inside drawn to the light outside; this is what they were made for. Startlings, too, carry this lucid hope: the lodestar of existence.

imagine
a stifling ignorance
falling away

The Startling

startle

– v.i.
to start
to undergo a start
to feel sudden alarm

– v.t.
to surprise as with fright
to cause to undergo a start
to take aback
to awake, excite

– n.
sudden alarm or surprise
startler

– adj.
startled

n. & adj.
startling

– *adv.*
startlingly

– *adj.*
startlish, startly

M.E. *stertle*
O.E. *steartlian*, to stumble, struggle, kick, or formed afresh, from *start*
M.E. *sterten*, closely akin to Du. *storten*, to plunge
Ger. *stürzen*

Surprise is a habit I hope I never grow out of. Every day I see something fresh, however many times I've looked. Like the way lisping, chuckling fieldfares are flung up in the sky, a flock of anchors. The accumulation of years and a self-questioning nature conspire to leave me threadbare, but I'm still propelled forward in a hurtle of curiosity and wonder; through binoculars, watch blue tits, as they peck and peck to stay alive, puff out their powder-yellow breasts.

Our habit of othering is deep-rooted. Despite myself, I am tricked into othering the future, as if it weren't my own and I had no part to play in breathing it into life. I am a Startling too. This heart, these two hands, these eyes are *startled*. I hear rabbits and weasels squealing among the trees behind the house: lives will be lost. Who wouldn't feel *sudden alarm*? It is at those who don't I am surprised; *taken aback* by the ones who turn away, choose not to notice that creatures and people and plants are dying.

I can smell wildfires, floodwaters, wake up with wet cinders on my pillow and rise to wash and begin again. Every day I *stumble, struggle*, find something to *kick* against – a wild thing tugging on a chain. But a small light at my core, a sequin made from birch bark, knows I am being *formed afresh* – myself and eight billion other sequins. Scales of the lavish, long-lived worldfish, we are ready to *plunge*. All of us in this time machine are Startlings.

> the future a foreign country
> where the language they speak
> is tenderness

Gamekeeper's Larder

The gate opens onto a muddy field. I'm drawn across the threshold by a regular grid of fine horizontals and pronounced verticals above the skyline – the unreadable calligraphy of an ancient accounting system.

Fifty-eight moles, pierced through their whiskery noses by each sharp knot of the barbed wire fence, their fur weathering away.

On the floor of my pantry, there's a mousetrap baited with a smudge of peanut butter to catch the mice who tunnel their way in, especially in winter, leaving droppings on the shelves, teeth marks in the vegetables.

I feel anxious at the mess they make, the invasion, and take recourse to a cull. Every so often, a mouse is killed, her neck broken by sprung steel. I must carry her small perfect body into the woods to be found by a buzzard or barn owl.

I stay long enough with the molecatcher's leavings to pay the debt of my attention, and to be affronted, repelled by my own righteousness. Where are my principles about interconnection and kindness when I load the mousetrap? A part of me eats itself up. Isn't this the way of it – the torque of paradox, the human trap: the ambivalent cost of living how we want, at the centre of things? We do our best, which is not good enough, imperfect, inconsistent, breaking our own hearts into little pieces.

This is the eye of the storm where we must live, make a home for ourselves, furnished with contradictions. We fail to encompass the stratigraphy of deep time and hold the future in our hands. Our imprint will live forever and we will die tomorrow. We are writing a story with no end.

> ask me where I live
> I'll show you a blade of grass
> the sharpening stone

Stagshaw Fair

At the crossroads I turn left and walk south, which I rarely do. Just past a plantation of Scots pine, the whole valley opens in a long yawn. Seeing further and wider, I am free, untethered from the domestic. From this perspective, everything is changed. Stone Meadow is a small footnote to Stagshaw Fair, keeping the secrets of centuries-long carousing close to its weather-beaten contours, an oasis of moss and tussock. Sometimes it's not always the closer you look the more you see. The farther back you step, the more your horizon shifts.

When I walk out the door I'm not beating the bounds of a neat rhomboid, a wedge-shaped patch of land pressed into the valley's highest point – a Roman soldier's bootprint magnified ten thousand, a hundred thousand times. I'm marking an X with my feet – a cross that tells me I am here, on a map of my own making. Standing in a different place, I can trace how the arms of the X stretch, unfurling the looped ribbons of a Möbius strip.

What I'd thought was a quadrat – boundaried, amenable to being named according to its parts – is in fact the sign for infinity. I am walking into endlessness. Going nowhere, I have plenty of time.

This land – I thought bled dry by years upon years of farming and trading, with its potholed roads and barbed wire fences, fizzing pylons, broken gates and discarded beer cans – keeps coming back to life.

It's getting dark. Houses in the distance send out dashes and dots of light, a scattered mosaic, and I am one small waterproof-jacketed sliver. As the shade deepens, the window lights square the circles of the stars, and I am pulled home from all directions.

life never speaks simply
it shows itself in its flower
it hides itself in its roots

The Glass Sponge

Another snowfall buries us in white, fragile and absorbent, muffling the sounds inside and out. We could be living underwater.

I first saw the skeleton of a glass sponge in an exhibition about Scott of the Antarctic. The delicate white forms left a paradoxical impression – like an articulation of light, both precise and ethereal. This particular variety was a Venus' Flower Basket, a symbol of enduring love in Japan, where it is often given as a wedding gift.

Some say the sponge, vase-shaped, luminous in deep water, is one of the planet's oldest living animals, the species 15,000 years old. I imagine the creature dying, leaving love behind in its six-pointed spicules, its lacy skeleton.

In its own time, the snow will leave spring behind. While I wait, I stay close to the fire, gathering all my lost ones around me. Together we make a small reef on the edge of a northern moor, where the weather and much else is unpredictable. Although my heart feels brittle, if I listen through the hushed layers, I know it's strong and intricate: built, like the love inside it, to last.

As well as a Startling, I am an Elder, a Rememberer. I remember the seasons that haven't happened yet. I remember everything I didn't know I knew.

here are the ones
who know how
to say thank you

O Hungry Moon

When you wake to snow every day, it is no longer a novelty, but you stay dazzled by the colours: blue, mauve, grey, silver and brown where the tractor's rolled through. There's nothing you want to do more than gaze at the wide plain of it, as if you were looking out to sea. We tell a child learning her colours that snow is white – the first of many lies she will take a lifetime to unlearn.

In this bardo between becomings, I'm trying to dream the future. It is like trying to dream God. There are those who would debate whether either exist. But all configurations long to be born and will find a way.

The snow is selfless, all colours and none, keeping the freezing air from the land where the seeds and shoots are stirring, unseen. In the soil, the future is already happening.

The shepherd rumbles past on his quad with a faint nod; otherwise I haven't seen a soul for days. The world, which I imagine is going on elsewhere, wants to divide us all into Withers and Withouters. I have a house to go home to, a tank full of propane, food in the fridge. I am a Wither. I admit the luxury of time to dream.

At the wooden sign for Heavenfield, I turn back, the snow too deep to go any further. In a field beside the track, sheep scrape at the snowy ground to crop the grass beneath.

dusk falls later
the hare still
then vanished

Countdown

I am not alone in having no words to speak about 'climate' or 'extinction'. These are abstract nouns buried in something made common. I keep on reading and writing about what I don't know, hoping I might find a path there. The page is full of empty space; it is the sky that fills the distances between birds. It is my mind blown open, with no idea of where the pieces will fall.

I don't know where mass extinction lives in my body, so I don't know how to live with mass extinction in my body. I carry it wherever I go, beyond the reach of language, unthinkable, radioactive, infectious.

My body walks in search of words born from disorder, decay, despair, scraps of birds torn from rotten branches. I practise seeing as an owl does, with circling vision, room for spaces between things. I pick up the broken alphabet, rearrange it in the dark and want to call it spring.

The moon is magnified through glass and I write by the light of it with old-fashioned ink. Like a mathematician, owl-eyed, I write 500. I write 187 and 11,147. In the past five hundred years, 187 of the world's 11,147 species of birds have gone extinct.

I write 500. I write 471. People who can see further have calculated that in the next five hundred years, three times as many – 471 species of birds – are in danger of going extinct. Always subtract, never multiply or add. The silver nib punches tiny holes in my heart. My ink runs out.

Everything I read and write is not about climate change; it is all climate change. Is this where we must live – between the lines, in negative space, our shadows blocking the light?

Truth is rare, endangered. Who tells you what counts?

> what light there is
> filtered through the fan
> of their feathers

Meteorological Spring

Even though the snow has gone, it's still there, under my skin. Limbo is a hard place to be: you look forward or back for a holdfast or foothold. For a full cycle, each season is shaped by a new loneliness, the world and its people receding like melting ice.

I stare at blurred photographs taken from the sea floor 900 metres beneath the Filchner–Ronne ice shelf on the Weddell Sea. Little lichenous hairs and mouths persist in the gloom, point towards the limits of what we know.

Scientists have discovered living organisms far beneath shelves of Antarctic ice where they thought nothing could survive. Worms, barnacles and sponges feed on plankton washed in from nearly a thousand miles away. The scientists' story about what lives must change.

Ernst Haeckel's drawings of *Hexactinellida* show microscopic forms, complex, geometric, like the patterns I made with my Spirograph set when I was a child. They could be seeds or snowflakes, diagrams of what you hope the future might look like – various, idiosyncratic, fertile. A monochromatic prospect waiting to be coloured in. Coralish, sci-fi, branched and twisting, whiskery, peculiar – adjectives slipping out of their nets.

Even now there are colours and creatures still to be discovered, life where we never expected it. Glass sponges thrive in the warmer waters that carry more plankton, support more companion species – marine isopods, juvenile starfish, brittle stars. When the sponges die, they leave behind silica mats, perfect habitat for crinoids, anemones, other sponges. Life continues.

We, too, are the glass sponges' companion species, each of us stronger and more vulnerable than we know. We coil together in the Stygian dark. This is what I think about in the absence of snow.

and to watch Time
teaches one
to sing

Weathered

I am exhausted after picking the bones of man-made global warming. They never come clean. I only manage to walk as far as the birch plantation. My legs weigh me down as if they belong to someone else, a pervasive alienation.

There's a small gap in the fence by the gate and I slip into this off-limits place where the deer browse. It's all sapling and tussock, hard walking; cottongrass puffs still just an idea in the spiked leaves rising from mounds swollen with moss. Washed-out plumes of it tuft and spread among a vast population of organic material. All the details, the clashing textures overwhelm me. If it weren't so wet, and I weren't so tired, I'd lie down and let myself sink, become part of it, twigs tangled in my hair.

Being tired is dangerous. It makes you afraid, less curious. When no one is listening, being tired is inevitable. I fall to my knees and bury my face in the moss, breathe in its stubbornness.

When you look at a landscape and think there's nothing there, there will be mosses. If you look for longer, you lose all track of time.

Because of its endless complex forms, moss could be the land-locked sponge in the Northern Hemisphere. From a different affinity with water, its surfaces are absorbent, and some species have a nerve. Modestly, miraculously, it draws down carbon and checks the land's propensity to flood.

Moss is medicine. It soothes me. Near the equinox, I want to draw down the planet's innate balance, but before anything else, must close my eyes, sleep. On a pillow of *Hypnum cupressiforme*, cypress-leaved plaitmoss, for a long time, sleep.

so many missed turns
and accidents
sometimes what we call arrival

The One You've Been Waiting For

The sky's the colour of a bruise: dirty violet with blooms of sulphurous yellow. My clothes are soaked, my body wet, immersed as I am in warm brackish water. I lower my legs and rise like a creature being born from the waves, and the surface of the lagoon reseals itself into stillness behind me.

Water up to my waist, I walk to the nearest shore, blinking in the strange half-glow. The edge of the lake squelches green with Sphagnum moss, a liminal element midway between earth and water. I pick my way across to firmer ground and shake myself like a dog scattering droplets in a pulsing sphere of prisms.

It's not clear where the path is. The old ways of getting from here to there have disappeared, lost beneath deep channels of peaty liquid. As I step forward cautiously, lightly as I can, the earth stretches away in a patchwork of gunmetal water and small reedy islands.

You are out of your element and everything is enlivening. Nothing left to lose, you keep walking through the labyrinth of islands you have no name for, letting the warm air dry you. You've woken up and you are the one you've been waiting for. This is the broken border, the drowned mire.

bear witness
hold uncertainty
love the world

Walking into the Wind

Their tattered tweed jacket is tied round the waist with a length of twisted sedge. Muddy brown against the Queen-of-Hearts-red skirt, all gathers and defiant splendour animating the muted palette of this amphibious place. The face isn't giving anything away – neither heavy nor light, old or young, male or female, outrageously human.

They say 'Welcome. We welcome you and every part of you.' And when they tell you their name, it sounds like the wind, a whistle, a sneeze. It might be Huish. You've left your name behind and can't for the life of you remember it. If it sounded like weather, it would be the open chord of snow after it's fallen. Your mouth unlocks a plump zero in this place where snow is apocryphal, a long-forgotten myth.

They punt the narrow boat, prow pointed like a heron's beak, through the channels, between islands, past constellations of wooden huts. Places of rest for the five-fingered ones, they tell you, the huts belong to no one in particular. This is common land. Common water. A fishy smell makes you think of the coast. The coast has come inland, they say. No more edges: it's all edge. And so there are fewer names. For no reason anyone can remember this place is called Rushing Water. Three times they say it: *Rushing Water, Rush in Water, Us and Water*. Same. Different. The name for a watery place

in the mouth of the wind, big gaps between their teeth for the air to breeze through.

hearing the stones
cry out
under the horizons

Biophilia

The wind's strong hands steer the boat towards an island planted with a hut painted kingfisher blue. You disembark and the ground feels surprisingly solid, your legs less so. Inside the hut thin mattresses are laid on a wooden frame. At a pot-bellied stove in the corner, Huish cooks up a meal of rice and greens, washed down with tea made with dried herbs from a battered caddy on the alcove shelf. It tastes of mint and drowned flowers, a summer meadow in full flood.

The hut walls are covered in paintings and patterns, portraits of humans and four-legged animals, all manner of birds. Most you don't recognise, perhaps imaginary. The pictures are illuminated with strings of what might be words in a script you can't read, composed of dots and triangles. Thoughts of the Lookbackers, they say, the ones who want life to be different from the way it is, to happen at a distance, classified and translated into coded signs and symbols. Bending their red-skirted backside in the direction of the wall, they let out a loud fart from one end and a laugh from the other. So much for the Lookbackers.

Are you one of them? Belly full of rice, you're not interested in the answer. On the nearest mattress, you curl up like a foetus.

                     close enough
                     to see the stars shine
                     on the bird's breast

                                                    Just So

Huish, or the wind, or whoever they are, has a black cat called
Wistful. You think that's what they said. She curls up against you
and you can smell her stickleback breath. The world feels closer than
it's ever been. Time and weather upended, you have everything you
need. You want to write Rilke's words (in the Roman alphabet, the
only one you know) on the painted wall, speckle the throat of a sweet
pink bird already landed there:

*And now we welcome the new year, full of things that have never
been.*

You don't want to be a Lookbacker. You can feel all the parts of
you passing through. If you weren't wearing your thick green coat,
you'd be transparent, curious as a mirror to see what isn't there yet,
creative as an engineer who can't help building something out of
nothing.

Back in the boat, the cat sits at the stern. Drifting down the water,
you become a silhouette – a passage between life and death – from
one moment to another. You don't know if this is what has never
been or what has always been. Nowhere leads to nowhere else.

                     a nest sculpted
                     from what's real
                     and what's possible

People are working in rice paddies where land and water meet. They are stooped over, dressed in waterproof boiler suits, purple, dusky as the sky. You can't see the sun, although you feel its warmth. The col--ours and the heat are theatrical, luxurious as the scales on a butterfly's wing; if it weren't so full of bravura, it would be frightening.

Some of the huts have thatched roofs, reedy hollows stippled with archipelagos of moss. Everything is aspiring to the condition of islands, dispersed, erratic, simultaneously single and multiple. The air of abandonment doesn't seem like neglect – more redolent of freedom, an inherent fractal wildness.

There are fewer people than you'd expect. They look up as you pass and wave. Some call out with the sound of the wind, whistles attenuating as they reach you. Huish grins and whistles back. Again, your expectation is subverted: what is attenuated feels abundant. What seems less – more – a collective effervescence, oceanic.

The sound of singing trails over the water, flutes and drumming percolate through the heavy air. Like no music you've ever heard, there's alchemy in it, and no stopping to listen to it. Huish keeps on punting, in and out of the island waterways. He hasn't asked where you want to go. Even so, you don't know where there is.

> *here, now, always –*
> *a condition of complete simplicity*
> *(costing not less than everything)*

The Narrow Road to the Archipelago

Almost noon, we went out on the boat again. After rowing about five miles across the water, we finally landed on what looked like a beach.

Huish kept saying Northumberisland was the most beautiful place in the northern country. And they'd seen it all. The south-east was open to the sea, a bay over seven miles wide, lapping with water.

There were more islands than anyone could count: some long and thin, like fingers pointing to heaven; some splayed catching the current; some clustered together in twos and threes, forking to the west or stretching to the east; some with little mounds, as if they were carrying babies on their backs.

Here and there pine trees were a deep green, branches sculpted by the salty wind into supple shapes like the bodies of dancers.

The beach was on the Island of Men; in fact, a stretch of terrain conjoined with the neighbouring land mass. We walked to see the stone where an old man used to sit and look at the sea. Among the pines, we saw the occasional hut where people lived in seclusion from the world. Smoke, smelling of needles, resin and cones, rose from small fires not far from their doors. We didn't see anyone, not even a ghost.

While we were there, the moon came out and shone on the water, painting a different picture.

Heading back to Rushing Water, we found a place to stop on the way – another hut with windows open onto wind and clouds. And so, we settled down to sleep. I wanted to write a few words to hold it in place, but all I could manage was to repeat its name until it faded away and my eyes closed.

Northumberisland
Northumberisland
Northumberisland

One afternoon in the woods, many years ago, a strange thing happened to my eyes. Or the light, or the trees. All three perhaps. Everything within my field of vision became blurred, merged. All the details of colour, shape, and texture stayed clear as glass. I blinked a few times but this new way of seeing persisted, accompanied by an upwelling of bliss that permeated my entire being. I couldn't stop smiling and wanted to laugh.

When I tried to tell my companion what I was seeing, he was disconcerted, not experiencing anything out of the ordinary himself. I saw him looking at me as if I was a long way away. I bent down to touch the moss and the heather, to check they were real – solid – as they used to be. The sun was shining and the plants were warm, the trunks of the trees warm, as another human body is warm. 'Look', I said, 'look how everything is connected, how we breathe in the light together. Can't you see?' My friend was embarrassed, wanted to keep walking.

This wasn't heat shimmer, though it felt like an oasis: immanence. The light was almost liquid. I was a long way away, and incredibly close.

It seemed to only last about five minutes. Although time was meaningless while it was happening. I don't know what 'it' was. I hesitate to say *my vision* – but life was never the same afterwards.

Time comes rushing in, like a deluge. I try hard to keep my head above water. But when it's safe, I lie on my back and float – like an island – and that feeling comes back. Rapture, I suppose, oneness. An enormous yes. Once you've been there, nothing can be the same again.

> *therefore choose life*
> *that both you*
> *and your seed shall live*

It never rains in films. Except to signal a dramatic moment. Wind never happens. Unless to herald a disaster. My life is an unfashionable film full of weather. Halfway through another year the land is mottled white with snaux – the artificial (*faux*) variety they use on film sets. It's as if the clouds have climbed out of the sky and lain down on the grass for a rest.

The sheep are shedding wool in great clumps, fleeces slipping off like clouts cast before May is out. The air smells greasy, ripe with lanolin. The weather has become woolly.

How long does it take sheep's wool to break down and go back to the earth? How many birds' nests would a field of fleece fill? What if I collected it up, like a woman gathering fog in a fairy tale, and brought it home to make a pillow? And what would you dream of if you laid your head on a pillow stuffed with sheep's wool you'd collected yourself from your own small patch?

There'd be no counting sheep or carbon or years remaining. Just a cloud of sheepish softness that joined all the flocks and let your flesh be grass. The film would be very slow, silent except for the sound of the wind.

global temperature rise
of 2.7 degrees predicted
by the end of the century

Anatomy Lesson

Ajahn Chah said *There is only one book worth reading – the book of your heart*. I am trying to read the book of my lungs. Be with my body breathing. It knows how it goes without me. Life: breath, the air we all share. Where what's inside and what's outside meet. After all these years, you still don't trust one breath will follow another.

Until you do – those blessed moments when you remember to take time to close your eyes and listen; exhale, sigh like a tree and the air changes around you.

The body's weather is heart and lungs. And isn't this how we see the world – from these bodies asking to be healed? And if we answered, would the world be healed? Did we ever know how to read the book of life?

Every day I walk out to be among trees. Our temple for remembering, for breathing with, belonging. Oxygen. Carbon dioxide. Gravity. Root. Weather. Water. Light.

> the long pilgrimage
> of these days
> becoming the path

The Deep End

In your dreams there is no weather, no hot nor cold, dark or light. It's shadowy, tending towards monochrome. If there were weather where dreams live, it would be like this. Rain. Buckets. Insistent as tinnitus. Biblical.

You are in fact in Eden. The infinity spiral has snapped and the time for walking round in looping circles is over. *Let me fall if I must fall*, said Baal Shem Tov. *The one I will become will catch me.* You're not sure how old you are any more. This is the future, and the weather is made of water, cousin of snow.

Over the moors, you cross the country's hobbled backbone before zigzagging down into the valley on the other side. As befits a land called Eden, its contours are softer, greener. Offspring of all that rain.

It's been falling all night and the water is high. Full pockets of sound, single drops and corrugated sheets, a quickening rush and swish, a roaring susurration. You are soaked to the skin, your only truly waterproof layer. You sense all two square metres of epidermis absorbing and shrivelling.

Thunder rumbles a long way off, like fear, tamped down, beneath the surface of what you know. Although weather is a story about air and atmosphere – 'things on high' – here, the *dea ex machina* is rain. The river is flowing – the fast, repetitive sound of it, portent of floods and disasters. The constant movement – vertical and horizontal – stirs the ground under your feet.

And yet it is all perfectly what-we-call-natural – the water cycle – we'd be nothing without it. This river god and his ancient rituals of immersion, baptism – a sign of life and fullness; invisible organisms, too many to count, longing to come into being and make more life. For life's own sake. Drips solid as stone, liquid so loud and cold you can't hold it.

puck   puck   puck   puck   lip   puck   lip

Glassy, startled, the land rises up. And you are here, in your skin, part of it. Away from home, home. In your element. The one you will become will catch you.

> how to translate
> our endless words
> into acts of love

DAWN CHORUS

While the Plough's still hard at work churning clouds –
clouds Turner would have loved, moody, fat –
a tawny owl's set on clocking off, strings
of silence plucked, the sound of a heart breaking
like glass. Cue to lift the lid off the dark
forest of this fairy tale we live: here
we sit like old pagans looking at the sky
as if it were a god dividing night
from day. 4 a.m. and all we can hear
is the stir of the wind, held breath, earth
not ready to exhale yet. This is the life
we normally sleep through, don't hear for the boil
and prowl of our own minds.

                         But the red birds
of morning begin to claim their territory.
The restless owl closes a door crying out
for a drop of oil, the rent air tacked back
together with song. Up on their perches,
invisible birds buzz with the wake-up call
of hormone and instinct, jostling for longest,
loudest, limberest. *Listen to me! Listen to me!*
I'm alive! Alive! Something to boast about
after the long night's fasting. Our first bird,
a robin – early riser, fierce defender. Soon,
the song thrush, piping his two notes; blackbird
rinsing his golden beak, polishing the ring
round his eye. Necessary to give voice to this
yearning to live and love and have your children
survive. 4.25, something different happens –

an inchoate elating – in strikes the first warbler,
our northern nightingale, the blackcap.
All the threads of sound spinning now
in a net around us. We are enchanted,
words fail us, we are all ears, caught in the net,
not knowing if what we're hearing is spaces
or strings. We are liquid, our edges
melting into music till we lose our 'I'ness
and we are song. Our little flock huddle,
warm hands round cups of tea in the chill
of what still doesn't qualify as morning.
The trilling and calling, squeaking and fluting
crashes in from all directions, so
the whole body is tender to it, our core
touched by it; a wood pigeon's aching purr,
distant falsetto. This is the way
you always wanted to begin the day – met
and held, lifted back into yourself
after the long night's forgetting. A small
interstice of feeling lost so you can fall
into finding why you're bone-alive again.
The erotics of ornithology:
living through the senses all the way to rapture,
joy. An hour of nothing else between
your ears and you can't stop grinning, mouth
widening to make more room for all this
glory, all this life for its own sake. 5.40,
nothing short of radiance, sun rising above
an elusive horizon, splashing trees,
walls, you, with gold, loud and sharp as the birds
singing so they become its guardians,
mystic visitants, spirits of the day.
Pheasant and wagtail, great tit and chiffchaff,

goldcrest and wren (little wren, who weighs less
than a 50p piece), treecreeper, blue tit
and mistle thrush (with his football rattle) –
an onomatopoeia of feathered things
that Emily Dickinson, dressed all in white,
heard as 'Hope', vowel and plosive, a gesture,
a giving of lips and throat –

                how we learned
to talk after all, by imitating
these birds, borrowing their beauty, bringing
our very selves to light. And so we hear the compass
of our own hearts – workshop and tinsel, too many
yesses to count; according to Emily, *find ecstasy
in life, the mere sense of living joy enough* –
turning it up, turning it up, us all, ratchet and caw.

THE TIME

Darkness will not be all that defines this new blink of landscape.
A sky of third-eye-indigo invites you to jettison – jump

right in. Your landing will be softened by unexpected slipstreams
of sheep's wool and lanolin; clock-shaped narcissism

replaced with a book of nights, stars, seeds
and spores, Fibonacci calendar of vegetal being.

First to rise is lichen, glaucous and antlered, sexual proclivities
pre-Linnaean, her 17,000 names as precious as anything – no, yes,

– everything you learnt at your desk or hearth,
or under your feet, in disguise, from the earth.

Ancient comrade darters bring word of change, cataclysmic,
unnegotiable – a low revolutionary arc

proving the worth of their failsafe faith
in flux: what time sees through a glass darkly – enough,

abundance – animal-vegetable-mineral's blessed alchemy.
The pattern of the formula of the dynamic (even

the correct designation beyond you) deepens like a pain at the back
of your reptilian neck escalating

up and down your mammalian spine, jarred by all that crashing
about you did in the '80s. The fractal mosaic

of the dragonfly's wing extends a glimmer
of precision, gentleness – not flight, a hoisting perhaps, aiming

in the right direction (towards a constellation yet to be identified)
alongside verdigris lichen,

which has no need to aim anywhere. Not a gun. And, though armed,
remember, neither are you, or your kind.

Nothing is not occurring – the lichen is also winged, inconspicuous,
aspirational. She has the power, natural symbiosis,

to teach you how to make friends
with the time, this moment – save your breath;

that knack she has of flinging her cups, her candles, her nets over
the world, catching it, and letting go.

A CURE FOR BLINDNESS

Only when they're empty
and raw do you discover
the cure in your hands.

>   In each palm an eye
>   sees what needs to be given,
>   a loaf, a lift, some folded notes,

shadowplay of touch.

>   When all you own, know
>   and love is what's asked,
>   your fingers threaten to break

with the whole earth's weight,
bones brittle with seeing
all this blind world needs,

>   every ounce of letting go.

Those eyes never blink – instead
shed small pearls of water
to rinse your unbound hands.

TENDERNESS

Which is our greatest strength
Which is love's most modest form

Which is Eros's necessary source
Which is the secret title of all poems

Which is the rule of life
Which is of and in the dove

Which is a cow deprived of their young
Which is a bruise that never goes away

Which is quiet and can't be heard
Which has no equal charm

Which is a mother's arms
Which is diamond incarnate

Which is the throat's sweetest music
Which is deeper than seduction

Which is relentless
Which is this life we share

Which is a gardener's patience
Crack rock and let the soul emerge

ARWEN

Oak, pine splintered to their white bones, fallen
        at tragic angles, as if the world itself were cracked

and shattered: think of the barn owls, the wide-winged one
        and the young one that light up the gloaming

where are they? And the stubborn beetles, horns
        upended, hurled into the wind, treeless and migrant

the daytime birds gentled by branch and bark and boon
        who sing them kin. Roots ripped out, worms and woodlice

exposed – all the juicy threads of mycorrhiza, fungi
        and snuffling creatures braided together, unstrung

so how can I not feel my own flesh felled, flailed, barren
        and broken? A tree tells me where I am, which way

to walk, but after the storm days have lost their drift.
        I don't know where I need to be. No boat or anchor

beached on foreign soil, I'm unhomed, unhearted
        uprooted, tangled and fibrous. A dry violence.

& BIRCH

Out of the silence, spores of woodland song answer
        the empty air, seeds can't help themselves but grow

courage and trust. Lovers of darkness, our pale roots
        will burrow down with animate tenacity and send out

rootlets, until the upward shoot spears lightwards
        pouring forth green and lenticel, vein and toothed edge

uncoiling pennons, time-lapsed sails to spiral us
        home. Meanwhile the birches will cast their nets

around me, where the deer roam and the hare leaps
        and the owls might seek shelter, what leaves are left

shiver like an old diva remembering her heyday
        wreathed in sequins. Those trees that survive

the storms are supple in trunk and limb. It is not
        of their nature to snap – it is their nature to throw

their arms up in bracelets of warm silver and cry
        begin again!   *again!*   *bless!*   *what next?*

MANDALA OF THE JAPANESE BEGONIA

First: contours, a map of a faraway
country, shoreline a riddle of inlets,
archipelagos I want to visit,
see the ground through the eyes on the soles
of my feet;
                close-up, you come into focus –

a narrow road, four leaves, clouds floating
low in the valley of morning.
                        Each frond,
veined with river deltas traced from the air,
lays bare a new direction, declares
another there is possible.
                    Today,
I linger where our compass points meet,

the heart's invisible engine:
                    sadness
joy   red   green –

    two sides of the same leaf.

TREE OF KNOWLEDGE

Unseasonable damp heat seeds spores,
a contagious grey pallor curls the tips of leaves

into fists. I cut off the mouldy shoots. We are
writing this poem together. Stray trusses stay

out of reach without tilting a shaky wooden ladder
against the snaking trunk to clamber into uncertainty.

A woman, no scholar of gravity, who planted a sapling
(*Saturn, Tree of Knowledge*) bought by post

from the British Library, I want the poem and its tree
to last longer, survive. The fruit's just starting to set,

downy thumbs of sweetness, apples-to-be, mildew
and artless balance willing. Inside the poem,

unrunged, inside nature, might we catch sight
of love and know where we live?

SEASONAL

language too inclining to rot –
     you hold each word up to the light

not to test for flaws
but to live inside

carry the stillness
of atoms colliding

     – a tree fruits
just before it dries

and sheds
goes home to winter

shouldering
its own bones

     how to sift
through the litter –

love this life
you crunch underfoot

and pass on

AXIS MUNDI

Whiskery tips to the branches and a gaunt
darkening in the leaves are a sign of disease.
There is writhe in the trunks, knuckle
and burr, a lost-wax grief to fissured bark.

This year the buds never looked more
mythological – pollen dusting everything
with gold. The god who can see the future's
hanging there and if we don't feel sorrow,

we might as well be dead. Underground,
the trees' sickness shares a root system
with my pathogenic rage. Its spores mist
my eyes so, walking through the tunnel of ash,

I see not light at the end but a twist
in the road, an impassable wall, gloaming.

BILBERRYING

Late July, evening is a door out of day.
At the end of the lane navy moons glint
darkly among a low sprawl of bushes.
I pick one, bruised with the bloom of summer
passing. Its bosky sweetness bursts on my tongue.

Kneeling with my plastic ice-cream tub, I am
a giant in a twiggy orchard, clumsy
compared with these tiny perfect things.

The picking takes forever and the bushes
go on forever, a miniature forest.

I am Psyche – bilberry picking at dusk
one of my interminable labours,
a rite of passage before I can enter
into anything like wholeness.

                    I'm too old for this.

My knees are sore, my arms are sore, aching
with the never-ending task. How do we make
a self, soul blown open, in this new fallen
world? How big are we? How small?

                    My hands are stained,
maroon ingrained in my fingers' whorls.

Glossy waves are washing beyond and towards me;
leaves surprised by crimson shouts, as if the fruits
were so hungry for life, for giving life back
to life, they're incarnate, foliate, blood.

They yell that the picking's never finished,
my tub will never be filled, and I runneth over –

return to the drover's road, dizzy
and ripe with imperfection. Two buzzards loop
overhead, mewing, kittenish, across deep blue.

NATURE-BASED SOLUTIONS

At the webinar propped on my kitchen table
  the minister asks us to consider (third in a list
   of six) *nature-based solutions* to the crisis
we find ourselves in for the very reason
  phrases like this are scattered like straws and clutched
   at, smoke rising from a house on fire. In this *window
to act*, he calls it, a *positive inflection point*, I try to think
  of a single thing that isn't based within nature –
   if that means part of us all and where we live, us
humans and our fellow creatures, flowers and trees,
  moss and mushrooms, not forgetting lichen, the dirt
   under my fingernails, perennial flora blooming
in my gut. Above my head there's a tap-tap-tapping
  like the woodpecker who sometimes mistakes our house

   for a tree. The roofer's fixing leaks round the chimney

and in the gulley between me and my neighbour.

  He took over his father's business but wouldn't want
   his son to: his body's *shot to hell* he says from all
the clambering and crouching and clinging he has to do
  on roofs all over the county. He's making a consummate job
   of it, handling every slate, anti-clockwise, with such care
they could be the armour of Marianne Moore's *near artichoke*,
  the pangolin, *scale lapping scale with spruce-cone regularity*.
   Up here the wind and the rain puff their cheeks

but we'll be okay now the roofer's doing what he does.
     He reminds me I have some nature-based solutions
            of my own. I open my mouth and start speaking
passionflower, all the words coming out like nails,
     pollen-dusted verbs and vowels mending what is broken,
       spreading seeds and changing with the weather.

CLIMATE CITIZENS' ASSEMBLY SHOW AND TELL

This view from the bedroom window.
My glasses.
Watch.
A money box.
A photograph of my daughter.
Single-use plastic.
A lump of coal.
The Union flag.
Car keys.
The cycle routes of Newcastle.
Telescope.
More photographs – her son, grandchildren, niece, the Swiss Alps,
our riverside walk, Planet Earth, a holiday snap,

a heart budding on a branch.

Dinosaur.
Book.
Placard.
Rock.
Here, this hawthorn tree.
A 100 Danish krone note.
His cycling helmet.
House keys.
Two indoor plants – one snake, the other fig.
A log.
Binoculars.
Knife.
A map of our region.
Camera and hourglass.
A packet of seeds.

THE NEARNESS OF THINGS

The subtle wings
of your words, your hands
on the shaded screen –

all day I stayed touched
by them – and the notion
of all you scientists

as you said, building
your own garden sheds
everyone's own little shed

when what was needed
was a Shard
so you had to shift

the way you worked –
what you studied
with your minds, your hands

the way you shared
your research
so you could build

a structure to rise
sheer above the horizon
beyond the impossible

and maybe that way
make a shelter
for the shuddering world

and did you know
a shard is also
a beetle's wing-case

a case it carries
when it must shed
the shadows of earth

and cast itself off
into the last shreds
of sunlight.

LATITUDE

Today the pond is the weather's eye.
It looks at you accusingly – enabler
of leaks and algae, neglecter of duties.

The skimmers skim and the boatmen row, bronze
athletes, at one with their reflections.

Virtuoso skaters spring onto
each other's backs in brief boleros
before they return to their solo grazing.

Submerged snails also feel the sudoku
of shells and soft bodies, multiplied spirals.

Little brown tongues of tadpoles, tremulous
with possibility, test the sound
of water and, for now, it is silence.

A newt scrambles among bones of leaves
on the drowned hills, splaying her lovely hands,

kimono of a tail rippling. One croaked hiss
rises in a plume of sweetness as if
the smallest hippopotamus in the world

were beached on the island of kingcups,
strewn with the old rowan's unstrung corals.

The sun is making this happen. It holds
the pond's gaze unswervingly, dispensing
spores of heat and light from its new

elevation, the ark of spring. Your role
is hitchhiker, fair weather gardener, pond twitcher.

AT UNTHANK

A dream of unbrainwashing, unsuicide
watching the three-by-sixers, cloud-tickers
unextract, unpollute, undestroy

by Fairleymay Gill, Yecklish Burn and Willow Letch.
Steel-ballerinas, spitfire-doodlers whisper
unbolt, unbetray, unbenight.

By Shotleyfield Burn, Mere Burn, Shortycroft Gill
earth-sails, weather-propellers, grey-riders
watershed-signers – the village sleeps through

their lullabies, unhungry, unhomeless, unterrified.
One by one the heron's-beak blades dip
and stop turning as an equinox wind unblows.

ON LIDDELLS LAND

These few hours, let's say we're in paradise.
The world outside doesn't climb the gate
to follow us in – no snakes in the long grass.

Charmed by goldfinches' yellow chatter,
we walk widening circles through the woodland,
marsh and meadow, sweetened into balance

by slow sunlight: the stridulations
of cryptic grasshoppers, wild raspberries,
hay rattle and *orchids! orchids! orchids!*

all the news we need. We watch a deer
steer her faun to a bolthole among pines.
Which side of the drystone wall is real?

Has the star-smudged enchanter's nightshade cast
its spell on us? An old curse of ignorance?
Or the gift of seeing beyond the dark?

We stay as long as we can, before coming
home past the high place where glaciers
once scarred the rock, inscribing their own fall.

TIMEFULNESS

time holds me so close to life
I can hear it breathing
and it's my breath

> we're a set of matryoshka dolls
> nested inside our mother
> and she's nested inside
> hers and hers and hers

> we carry the future nested
> inside us twenty-two thousand
> breaths every calendar day

I wake in a room
where I can measure the horizon
what weather sky holds

standing on Stagshaw Fair
the past rises through my feet

> part-human part-digital part-plastic
> I try to keep my bad wiring earthed

in stiff-legged drifts sheep
are reliable companions
but comfortless – after forty years
I'm no closer to understanding
however hard I stare into the blank
rectangles at the centre of their eyes

the albino pheasant
scurries for cover
when I try to creep close enough
to see his eyes
leucistic black or true pink

                              at either end of the field
                                    gates clang shut
                              galvanised quotation marks

pond boulders are remnants of forever
cast-offs from Hadrian's Wall
nearly two thousand years old

at Heavenfield – a battle and a cross
yew trees candle the churchyard

and those six months cut loose in India
a hill town blanket's barcode stripes
gladdening my chilled knees
the cracks in my lumbar vertebrae

I lie flat like a stone kicked up
by the horse's hooves
tossing me out of my 37th birthday

                              stay close to the fire in winter
                                 throw on logs I gather
                              like my ancestors before me

watch the children growing
older – the blank currency of the moon
spent and saved – trees felled
and fallen wind blows through

                              in ten years I'll be the age
                              my mother was when she died

sky the colour
of a pigeon's breast
we fold ourselves
into the mutual

STONE MEADOW BOOK OF THE DEAD

A golden shovel after Audre Lorde

Every night the nuns chant *Do not squander your life*. I'm
thinking of painting it on my ceiling. You're going
to read it across the horizon of these lines to

remind you that time is what you're made of. It will go
quick as a spotted cat. Count your nine lives running out
and live the same way you want to die, zero waste, like

a flower that might be mistaken for a firework, a
wraith, flame-eater, fate-spinner, bucket-kicker, fucking
hell, imagine going out, like her, a meteor.

THE OCTOPUS MOTHER

after laying her clutch
                of a hundred thousand eggs,
      small as grains of rice,

watches over them
                the semi-transparent hatchlings
and ever so slowly disintegrates

until she is food
                devoured by her young
the first of all meals

just as past becomes future,
                the mother turns into what happens

      this is the trick of life

          we forget
                as we leak
          poisons into our bodies
and our children's
                the planet's amniotic oceans

IMMORTELLE

With nowhere else to go,

I wish for you the gift

of jellyfish silk – a bloom

to slow down your falling,

or is it floating, between

the elements to cup you

as you land like a seed

in the earth, an immortelle.

NOTES

'Le Temps I' is composed from a solitary year renga, verses written daily throughout 2021. It contains direct quotations (re-lineated, in italics) from Eugenio Montale (*It is only in ashes / that a story endures / only the extinguished persists*), Laurie Anderson (*a beginning that hasn't / even begun to begin*), Moshe Feldenkrais (*making the impossible possible / the possible easy / and the easy elegant*), Octavia Butler (*all that you touch you change / all that you change changes you / the only lasting truth is change*) and Henrik Blind (*our culture / written in snow / and the planet's on fire*).

'Le Temps II' is composed from a solitary year renga, verses written daily throughout 2020. It contains direct quotations (re-lineated, in italics) from Jane Hirshfield (*a moment knows / something's almost over / but not what it is*), Donna Haraway (*stay with the ragged joy / of ordinary living / and dying*) and Siri Hustvedt (*the here and now / and the mental there and elsewhere*). *Do not stand / in a place of danger / trusting in miracles* is a traditional Moroccan proverb.

'Stone Meadow Orbital' borrows the haibun form of Bashō's *The Narrow Road to the Deep North*. 'The Narrow Road to the Archipelago' is a version of his 'Matsushima' section in that work. Re-lineated fragments are included from Barry Lopez (*imagine / a stifling ignorance / falling away*), Luce Irigaray (*life never speaks simply / it shows itself in its flower / it hides itself in its roots*), Robin Wall Kimmerer (*here are the ones / who know how / to say thank you*), Hope Mirrlees (*and to watch Time / teaches one / to sing*), Ted Hughes (*hearing the stones / cry out / under the horizons*), T. S. Eliot (*here, now, always – / a condition of complete simplicity / (costing not less than everything)*), my own variation on Bashō (*Northumberisland / Northumberisland / Northumberisland*) and Deuteronomy (*therefore choose life / that both you / and your seed shall live*).

'Tenderness' is a cento made with variations on lines by (in order of appearance) Rumi, Olga Tokarczuk, Rollo May, Galway Kinnell, Pope Francis, Martin Luther King Junior, Thomas de Quincey, Phillip Pullman, Anna Akhmatova, Jane Austen, Victor Hugo, Han Suyin, Michel Houellebecq, William James, Pablo Neruda, Pema Chödrön, Ralph Fiennes and another from Rumi.

The Anderson quotation is from *Spending the War Without You*, Norton Lectures (2021). The Blind quotation is from 'This new snow has no name: Sami reindeer herders face climate disaster', *The Guardian* (2021). The Hustvedt quotation is from 'This living hand', *The Guardian* (2009). Montale is quoted with permission from Oberlin College Press, Feldenkrais from HarperCollins, Hirshfield from Bloodaxe Books and Penguin Random House, Haraway from Duke University Press, Irigaray from Bloomsbury, Mirrlees from Orion, Hughes and Eliot from Faber and Faber, Rilke from W. W. Norton & Co. The Merton epigraph, from *Turning Toward the World: The Journals of Thomas Merton*, Vol. 4, 1960–1963, ed. V. A. Kramer, is included with permission from The Merton Legacy Trust/Harper Collins.

ACKNOWLEDGMENTS

This work would not have been possible without the support of New Writing North, Newcastle University and Arts Council England. The University's Anthropocene Research Group, North of Tyne Combined Authority, Hexham Book Festival and Active Hope Training provided helpful forums for research and exchange. The book has benefited from careful and creative editing by Kate Simpson and skilful design and management by Faber and Hamish Ironside. I am very grateful to them all.

Thank you to the editors, judges and producers for the places where earlier versions of poems have appeared: *Dark Mountain Journal*, *Songs of Place and Time: Birdsong and the Dawn Chorus in Natural History and the Arts*, *dhamma moon*, Ginkgo Prize for Eco-poetry, *Gone Cuckoo*, *In Our Element* podcast, Manchester Poetry Prize, NCLA: *Inside Writing*, *Out of Time: Poetry from the Climate Emergency*, *poeticabotanica* blog, *The Alchemy Spoon*, *Under the Radar*, *You are Her*.

'Lightning Stone' is for Malcolm Green, 'Hearth' for Matilda Bevan, 'Incunabula' for Susan Williams, 'The Nearness of Things' for Muzlifah Haniffa (and the Human Cell Atlas), and 'Immortelle' is for Birtley Aris (1928–2021).

Warmest thanks for encouragement and insightful first reading of poems in progress to Cynthia Fuller, Matilda Bevan, Ajahns Sucitto and Abhinando.